W9-AFQ-124

TECH PIONEERS™

GRACE MURRAY HOPPER

ERIN STALEY

ROSEN
PUBLISHING

NEW YORK

Published in 2016 by The Rosen Publishing Group, Inc.
29 East 21st Street, New York, NY 10010

First Edition

Library of Congress Cataloging-in-Publication Data

Staley, Erin, author.
 Grace Murray Hopper / Erin Staley. -- First Edition.
    pages cm. -- (Tech pioneers)
 Includes bibliographical references and index.
 ISBN 978-1-4994-6288-3 (library bound)
 1. Hopper, Grace Murray--Juvenile literature. 2. Admirals--United States--Biography--Juvenile literature. 3. Women admirals--United States--Biography--Juvenile literature. 4. Computer engineers--United States--Biography--Juvenile literature. 5. Women computer engineers--United States--Biography--Juvenile literature. I. Title.
 V63.H66S73 2015
 359.0092--dc23
 [B]

                                                                    2015033180

Manufactured in the United States of America

Contents

INTRODUCTION

Video chatting with a friend, uploading music, posting a favorite vacation image, or streaming a blockbuster movie—technology has brought convenience and entertainment to our day-to-day lives. But it's difficult to imagine a time before computers and mobile devices. Thanks to the pioneering efforts of early computer scientists, we are able to connect with the world around us and embrace an always-changing technological industry.

One such pioneer was Grace Murray Hopper. She was a professor, military leader, and computer programmer. She worked during a time when computer science was more of a discipline than a career option. This was especially true for women.

As a child, Grace Hopper was naturally inquisitive. She loved gadgetry and, at seven years of age, was known for dismantling alarm clocks. She eventually earned advanced college degrees and became a professor of mathematics and physics. When the military base at Pearl Harbor was

Commodore Grace Hopper—a pioneer in software development and programming languages—believed her greatest achievement was inspiring future generations.

bombed in 1941, Hopper jumped at the opportunity to serve in a new way. She became a navy reservist and joined teams of computer scientists and engineers who were developing early computers. Their collaboration contributed to the United States' victory in World War II.

Hopper's career was both long and decorated. She made significant military and private industry developments. For example, she worked on early computers, including the Harvard Mark I and the UNIVAC. In an effort to make programming more user-friendly, she created the world's first compiler. It was a program that translated "high-level" language that humans could understand into "low-level" language that computers could understand. This development led to the creation of Common Business-Oriented Language (COBOL). Revolutionary in the computer industry, the program allowed computers to respond to words rather than numbers. COBOL continues to be in use today. Hopper also crafted software development ideas, and worked on compiler verification and data processing elements.

Hopper's work benefited the military as well as industry and academia. She even popularized the phrase "debugging," thanks to a moth that got stuck inside a large computer relay and had to be removed. Hopper's collection of professional achievements earned her the nickname the "Mother of Computing."

Although Hopper had established her reputation and received a slew of medals and honorary doctorates, her journey wasn't easy. She faced many challenges, such as a failed college entrance exam, rejection from the military, divorce, a no-nonsense boss, the challenges of being a woman in a male-dominated industry, and the need to "sell" her ideas to industry leaders. But Hopper was spirited. Her success was a result of her highly developed teaching and technical skills, diplomacy, and a thinking-outside-the-box approach to technology.

Grace Murray Hopper's life, both personally and professionally, is fascinating. She lived in a world where women were expected to fulfill traditional roles, but Hopper refused to conform. She pushed the limits of what it was possible for women to do professionally and in the military. She opened the pathway to young people today interested in a career in computer science. After all, Hopper believed her greatest accomplishment was inspiring young people to program. She challenged them to dig into the endless possibilities of technology and to ignore the "we've always done it that way" mentality.

Chapter One

MEET GRACE

The field of computer science has long been dominated by men. However, female pioneers have also made invaluable contributions to this rapidly changing industry. Their names—and amazing achievements—may not be as common as those of Bill Gates and Steve Jobs, but without them, we wouldn't have the technology we rely on today. "Everyone tends to make the joke that women in computer science are like unicorns; we kind of just don't exist," said one attendee to the 2014 Grace Hopper Celebration, interviewed for the ESPN-produced short film *Signals: The Queen of Code*, a biography of Grace Murray Hopper. But female computer scientists do exist, and the most notable of these so-called unicorns is Grace Murray Hopper.

A COMPUTER PIONEER IS BORN

Grace Brewster Murray was born on December 9, 1906, in New York, New York. Her father, Walter Fletcher Murray, was a local insurance broker. Her mother, Mary Campbell Van Horne Murray, was a homemaker. Grace was named after her mother's best friend, Grace Brewster. She was also the eldest child in her family. Grace had a younger sister, Mary, and a younger brother, Roger.

This Italian neighborhood market in New York, New York, offers a glance of big city living in the early 1900s.

The Murray children enjoyed a happy childhood. Young Grace was both studious and active. She was an avid reader, and had been taught needlepoint, cross-stitch, and piano by her mother. Grace also loved the outdoors, spending summers at the Murray family cottage on Lake Wentworth in Wolfeboro, New Hampshire. It was here where, in 1923, Grace would later meet the man who would become her husband. Kick-the-can, hide-and-seek, and cops-and-robbers—Grace played them all. Joining her and her siblings were lots of cousins. However, as the elder Murray daughter, Grace was expected to be the most responsible sibling. One day, while scrambling up a tree with the other children, Grace climbed the highest. However, she was also pointed out as the instigator. Grace was grounded from all swimming privileges for a full week.

A CURIOUS GRACE

Curious as a youngster, Grace had inherited her mother's passion for mathematics. Grace's mother had grown up in the late 1800s, a time when women didn't study math seriously. When they did, it was only to learn how to help manage household finances. However, Grace's grand-father, John Van Horne, thought differently. Van Horne had been a New York City senior civil engineer. He used mathematical skills in his profession every day. He often took his daughter (Grace's mother) on surveying trips and made it possible for her to study geometry. As unique as this opportunity was, the young Mrs. Murray wasn't able to take algebra and trigonometry classes—something that stuck with her into adulthood. When she became a mother herself, she encouraged both Grace and Grace's sister, Mary, to take full advantage of every academic opportunity.

From a young age, Grace Murray was fascinated by all things mechanical. As a seven-year-old, she was particularly interested in the old-fashioned alarm clocks of her family's cottage. There was one in each bedroom—seven to be exact. Curious about the inner workings, Grace dismantled one alarm clock. But she was unable to reassemble it. Instead of asking her parents for help, she took apart a second alarm clock. She still couldn't figure out the reassembly. Grace moved from room to room and clock to clock, until her mother intervened. One alarm clock would be all the child was allowed to play with. This mechanical curiosity continued throughout Grace's adolescence and well into her celebrated career as a tech pioneer.

EDUCATIONAL EQUALITY

Despite societal norms, the Murrays wanted their daughters, Grace and Mary, to have the same educational opportunities as their son, Roger. Grace's for-

PROGRESSIVE WOMEN

Before the twentieth century, women were very limited in their educational and professional options. In general, they were expected to be homemakers. They raised the children, tended to their husbands and elderly relatives, and volunteered for community causes. Educational curricula for women included only those subjects that would help them be successful in these more traditional roles. Advanced materials such as physics and mathematics were reserved exclusively for their male counterparts.

At the turn of the twentieth century, women began demanding equal rights. They started to shed stereotypes that portrayed them as frail and modest. Women sought new opportunities in education, hiked up their hemlines, cut their hair, danced in public venues, and worked outside the home. This shake-up occurred in what is commonly referred to as the Progressive Era (1890–1930). When the United States joined World War I in 1917, men were called away to battle. This left many jobs unfilled. Women were needed to serve as conductors, postal workers, bank tellers, police officers, and firefighters. They made weaponry for the war, guided heavy machinery, and labored on farms across the country. They also made noteworthy contributions to male-dominated fields, such as science, literature, engineering, medicine, and politics. In the 1920s, the number of American women working outside the home increased to nearly 50 percent. With each

Women left more traditional roles in order to work at bomb factories during World War I. Their efforts were instrumental in securing a victory and advancing women's rights.

passing decade, women have made further advances and received greater recognition for their contributions to society. Today, there are more opportunities for smart and hardworking women than ever before.

mal education began at the Graham School. It was just a few blocks from the Murray's New York City home. The Graham School was a well-known private institution for girls. It emphasized the "hows": how to study, how to think on one's own, and how to fulfill one's personal duty. The school's mission was to foster academic enjoyment, to awaken the students' enthusiasm, and to help them improve their opportunities. Hopper attended the Graham School from 1911 to 1913.

In 1913, Grace was enrolled in Miss Mary Schoonmaker's School for Girls. It was also in New York City. It developed girls into women under the motto: "Self Respect, Self Control, Self Reliance." Beyond a full academic load, Grace continued to be as active in her adolescence as she was in her childhood. She played basketball, field hockey, and water polo. However, when it came to preparing for her college of choice, Vassar College in Poughkeepsie, New York, she wasn't successful. Grace failed a Latin exam. She was advised to wait a year before reapplying. Her parents agreed. At sixteen, they thought she was too young for college. Instead, Grace enrolled in the Hartridge School in Plainfield, New Jersey, in the fall of 1923. She graduated in 1924. That September, she reapplied to Vassar. This time, she was accepted. Grace studied mathematics and physics as well as beginning sciences, business, and economics. She also sought out adventures such as buying a ride on a one-engine biplane. It was made from wood, linen, and wire. She spent all of her money at the time—a total of $10—to feel the full force of the wind from the open cockpit.

By 1928, Murray had graduated with a bachelor's degree in mathematics and physics. She was also elected to Phi Beta Kappa, the oldest and most prestigious honors society in the United States. Murray was then awarded a Vassar College Fellowship (1928–1929) to continue her education. This allowed her to focus on her studies, instead of working full-time. She later earned a Sterling Scholarship (1929–1930) to pursue her educational goals further at Yale University in New Haven, Connecticut. It had been her father's alma mater. He graduated in 1894. Grace Murray earned a masters degree in mathematics and physics from Yale in 1930.

Yale University is the third oldest US university. Among other famous alumni (including inventor Eli Whitney and several former presidents) is Grace Hopper.

MARRIAGE AND ADULTHOOD

Not only did Murray gain a masters degree in 1930, but she also gained a husband. She married Vincent Foster Hopper. He was a Princeton University graduate, having received his masters degree in 1928. Murray and Hopper said, "I do" on June 15, 1930. At the time of the Hopper wedding, Vincent was teaching English in New York University's School of Commerce, Accounts, and Finance (known today as the Leonard N. Stern School of Business).

The Hoppers honeymooned in Europe. They traveled to England, Scotland, Wales, and France. Upon their return, the newlyweds settled in New York City. He taught locally, and she accepted a position teaching at Vassar College. It was about a two-hour train ride away from their home. Hopper became an assistant instructor in mathematics and taught algebra, calculus, and trigonometry. She later added analytics, statistics, and theory of probability to her teaching schedule. But Hopper wasn't like other math professors. She wanted her students to be as skilled at writing as they were at calculating numbers. In one particular case, she asked students in her probability course to write an essay about one of her favorite mathematical formulas. Once they were handed in, she marked them up. When faced with criticism that her students were there for math and not

Richard Courant (1888–1972) fled the rise of the Nazi Party in his native Germany in 1933. He later became a professor at New York University. Courant cofounded The Courant Institute of Mathematical Sciences.

English, she explained that it was pointless to master math without being able to communicate it properly to others. This was a belief that Hopper carried with her throughout her long career.

As a professor, Grace Hopper earned $800 a year. This was a lot of money back then, especially after the American stock market crash of 1929. The Great Depression (1929–1939) followed, and many Americans lost their jobs. In fact, the average annual income was only $1,970. Having a consistent paycheck allowed one to buy a pound of steak for twenty cents, a gallon of gas for ten cents, a new car for $640, and a new house for $7,145.

While Hopper taught at Vassar, she also pursued a Ph.D. in mathematics and physics at Yale University. She studied under the tutelage of Norwegian mathematician Øystein Ore (1899–1968). He was known for graph theory, a branch of mathematics that studies points and lines. In 1934, Grace Hopper earned her PhD. In 1939, the Hoppers built a two-story home in Poughkeepsie, New York. She continued to teach at Vassar, but by 1940, she took a partial leave to study with Richard Courant at New York University. He was a well-known mathematician who focused on methods to solve partial differential equations using finite differences. That same year, the Hoppers separated. They later divorced in 1945. They did not have children. Hopper never remarried, but chose to keep her married name.

Chapter Two

MAKING A MARK

G race Hopper was just a child during the First World War (1914–1919), but the whole world—children included—paid attention to the key political issues and latest news from the war front. At the time, World War I was the deadliest global conflict in history. The world watched as the greatest devastation ever witnessed occurred. In 1919, peace was reached, and the Treaty of Versailles ended the war between the Allies (including the United States) and the Central Powers (Germany, Austria-Hungary, and the Ottoman Empire).

LINGERING RESENTMENT

Nearly two decades had passed since the signing of the Treaty of Versailles, and unsettled disputes among

THE LEAGUE OF NATIONS

The Treaty of Versailles required Germany to take complete responsibility for World War I. Germany was also ordered to limit its armed forces, give up colonies and territories to Allied nations, and pay $33 billion to other nations that had suffered great loss. The treaty also established the League of Nations (which lasted from 1920 until 1946). This organization was designed to prevent a second world war by giving countries—no matter their size—a voice to negotiate with each other. If attacked, the others would impose sanctions on the offender. Sanctions were a formal decree that limited or stopped all trade and aid to an offending country. This would be devastating as many nations relied on imported food and supplies.

Forty-eight countries signed the Treaty of Versailles on June 28, 1919. However, the United States was not one of them. President Woodrow Wilson (president from 1913 until 1921), who had developed the idea for the League of Nations, decided that it was best to let European nations tend their own affairs. The United States did honor the Treaty of Versailles, with the exception of the creation of the League of Nations. It also created a separate treaty with Germany called the Treaty of Berlin (1921).

Unfortunately, the League of Nations did not have a military force. It could not back up the sanctions and was, in essence, powerless in times of hostility. The

League of Nations faded in importance and officially disbanded after World War II. The concept remained, however, and later evolved into the United Nations, which still exists today.

nations remained. Germany, in particular, had lost one-sixth of its territory, and was deeply in debt. Like other nations, it was also affected by the Great Depression of the 1930s. Jobs were scarce, and inflation was out of control. The German people were frustrated, angry, and in search of a leader who could fix the nation. A charismatic leader by the name of Adolf Hitler stepped up to the challenge. He quickly rose to power, and established the National Socialist German Workers' Party. Also known as the Nazi Party, this political group helped develop and enforce Hitler's nationalist agenda. Hitler blamed the Jewish people for Germany's misfortunes, and the Nazis began an appalling anti-Semitic campaign. Hitler also set up a totalitarian government under the guise of restoring the former greatness of Germany. His plan was to slowly conquer Europe and expand German borders and resources. He rejected the Treaty of Versailles and began invading other countries. The League of Nations was powerless to respond. However, when Germany invaded Poland on September 3, 1939, Great Britain and France declared war on the hostile nation. World War II had officially begun.

Meanwhile, in Italy, longtime fascist dictator Benito Mussolini had stabilized his nation's economy. He had also set up public programs. But these improvements came at a great price for his countrymen. Free press and trade unions were illegal, freedom of speech was squelched, and a web of spies and secret police kept a watchful eye over Italian citizens. Mussolini also expanded his empire with foreign conquests. In October 1935, when Italy brutally attacked the African nation of Abyssinia—now called Ethiopia—the League of Nations condemned Italy's actions. It imposed sanctions, keeping exports from leaving the country and supplies from entering. Mussolini turned to Adolf Hitler for help. The two signed the Pact of Steel on May 22, 1939. It was an agreement that if one went to war, the other would come to its aid.

JAPAN AND PEARL HARBOR

While Germany swept across Europe with victories, Emperor Hirohito of Japan considered his own empire. He had longed for expansion in Southeast Asia and in the Pacific, part of a Japanese political trend known as Statism. Despite being a member of the League of Nations, Japan invaded fellow member China. Furthermore, the vulnerable Pacific colonies administered by just defeated

European Allied nations were too appealing for Japan's surge of expansionism. These colonies had the raw materials—petroleum, rubber, and tin—needed to help Japan become self-sufficient and, thus, more powerful. In 1940, Japan invaded northern Indochina. Germany and Italy applauded Japan's efforts. The three nations signed the Tripartite Pact on September 27, 1940. It was an agreement that guaranteed economic, military, and political aid to its participants.

When Japan advanced southward in the Pacific, the United States responded by putting a freeze on Japanese assets. It also placed an embargo on oil. However, Allied

Most of the damage from the Pearl Harbor attack occurred within the first thirty minutes. Pictured are two battered vessels, the USS *West Virginia* and the USS *Tennessee*.

forces were weak. Japan took the opportunity to build a defensive boundary around its interests. An aggressive strategy was put into place, and on December 7, 1941, Japanese fighter planes bombed the US Pacific Fleet at Pearl Harbor in Hawaii. The attack lasted for two hours; 2,500 people were killed. A thousand more were wounded. Eighteen ships and almost three hundred planes were damaged or destroyed. Americans were outraged. The United States declared war the following day. Troops were sent to Europe, North Africa, and the Pacific. Germany and Italy declared war on the United States on December 11, 1941.

Patriotism and Grace

When Pearl Harbor was attacked, Americans banded together. Thousands joined the war effort. Hopper's husband and family were among them. Grace Murray Hopper's then husband Vincent Hopper volunteered for the US Army Air Force, as did Grace's brother. Her father served on the Selective Service Board, a government agency that drafted men into the military. Hopper's mother took a position on the local Ration Board, an organization that made sure every American got their fair share of short-supply goods. These included meat, sugar, butter, nylon, silk, shoes, gasoline, tires, and chicken wire fencing. Hopper's sister went to work in a General Electric factory to make bomb fuses.

Hopper advocated for progress in computer science. She loathed the words, "We've always done it this way," and championed innovation.

Grace Hopper decided to join the US Navy because her great-grandfather, Alexander Weston Russell, had been a rear admiral. However, she did not pass the physical. For her height of 5 feet 6 inches (167 cm), the navy required that she weigh 140 pounds (63.5 kilograms). Hopper weighed in at 105 pounds (47.6 kg). Plus, she was thirty-seven years old, too old for the reserves. Hopper's position as an associate professor of mathematics at Vassar College played into their decision as well. She was thought to be more helpful to the war effort as a civilian. Never one to give up, Hopper pushed until she got what she wanted. She received a waiver for the weight restriction and a special leave of absence from her teaching position. In December 1943, Hopper was sworn into the navy's Women Accepted for Voluntary Emergency Service (WAVES).

MAKING WAVES

After the attack on Pearl Harbor, military men were needed on the seas. This meant that women had to step in to more traditional male roles, including in the military. Women had enlisted in the Women's Auxiliary Army Corps (WAAC) when there was a need during World War I. They served as nurses and yeomen. They were not commissioned officers. With World War II, however, the country needed to create a naval organization for female soldiers. On July 30, 1942, President Franklin D. Roosevelt signed Public Law 689 into effect. It allowed women to enlist in the navy's newly formed WAVES division. It also commissioned female officers. The response was overwhelming—1,993 female reservists signed up for the first WAVES regiment. An additional 1,600 to 1,700 women joined every two weeks. At the height of their efforts in 1945, over 104,000 women had served as WAVES reservists. Within three years, they made up 18 percent of the total naval force at home.

WAVES learned naval customs, etiquette, and discipline. Drills began with a singing session with the group, followed by a review of fundamentals and war front updates. Their jobs ranged from cryptologists and draftsmen to translators and instructors for male pilots-in-training. The WAVES program was so successful, it opened up more doors for women to serve in the US military. The Women's Armed Forces Integration Act (1948) allowed women to bypass special reserves such as WAAC and WAVES and enlist directly in the US military. Today, women serve in every military branch, protecting US interests on land, in the sea, and in the air.

A WAR OF SCIENCE

From May to June 1944, Hopper attended the Midshipman's School at Smith College in Northampton, Massachusetts. Not only was she older than her fellow recruits, but she realized that she would have to relearn how to memorize. It didn't take long for Hopper to figure it out, because she was commissioned a lieutenant junior grade on June 27, 1944.

"World War II was a war of science," says Kurt Beyer, Hopper's biographer, in *Signals: The Queen of Code*. He continues, "in order to have a war of science, it becomes a

Grace Hopper was passionate about her inventions and what they could do for users, both in the computer science industry and beyond.

war of mathematics as well. So some of the most important problems that needed to be solved were ballistics tables." Women were hired to break down the problems, and calculate the ballistics trajectories by hand. These women were called "computers." Because of her mathematical background, Grace Hopper was assigned to work on a secret project. It was the Bureau of Ordnance's Computation Project at Harvard University. On her first day in July 1944, she was greeted in the most unusual way by her new boss, Howard H. Aiken. He was known for his fiery leadership style. Hopper describes Aiken's first words to her: "'Where the hell have you been?' He then waved his hand at Harvard Mark I, all fifty-one feet of her, and he said, 'That's a computing engine!'"

Hopper was smitten—by Harvard Mark I, that is. "I always loved a good gadget," she said, as quoted by Anne B. Keating and Joseph R. Hargitai in the book *The Wired Professor*. "When I met Mark I, it was the biggest fanciest gadget I'd ever seen . . . It was fifty-one feet long, eight feet high, eight feet deep, and could perform three additions per second . . . I had to find out how it worked." Mark I was massive; it weighed five tons. Inside, over 750,000 parts hummed twenty-four hours a day, seven days a week. It contained 3,000 decimal storage wheels, 1,400 rotary dial switches, and 530 miles of wire with three million wire connections. Its input system was paper tape with punched code that ran through the computing engine.

HOWARD H. AIKEN

Howard H. Aiken (1900–1973)—an electrical engineer, physicist, and scientist—was the brains behind Mark I. He had been a graduate student in physics at Harvard University. While working on his dissertation in 1937, he longed for an electromechanical computing device that would do all of the tiresome calculations. Aiken designed a solution. It was a computing engine called the Harvard Mark I.

When the United States entered World War II, Aiken went to work for the navy. He knew Mark I could be useful with atomic physics, optics and electronics, and radio research. Aiken became a commander and ran the project like a military operation. Mark I was his ship, and Hopper—much to his dismay, because she was a woman—was his second in command. Aiken was tough and demanded fast, accurate, and reliable results from his hard-working team. However, he saw that Hopper was very loyal—a quality which he admired. Hopper eventually won Commander Aiken over, and he relied heavily on her wisdom, skill, and diplomacy.

Grace Hopper and Richard Bloch (1921–2000) alternated twelve-hour shifts to program the temperamental Harvard Mark I, shown here at Harvard University.

ON-THE-JOB TRAINING

While Hopper was knowledgeable about mathematics and physics, she lacked essential programming know-how. Hopper would need to learn many of these programming skills on the job. "Everything was hurry up, do it yesterday," says Hopper in *Signals: The Queen of Code*. Biographer Kathleen Williams makes the following observation in her book, *Grace Hopper: Admiral of the Cyber Sea:*

It is a testament to Hopper's toughness that she was not rattled by her first encounter with Aiken. In fact she quickly came to respect him and to regard him very highly, although she did refer to those early days as her "sufferings." She freely admitted that she would not have accomplished the task Aiken so abruptly assigned to her on the first day without the help of the whole crew.

Hopper's on-the-job training didn't come easily. Misogyny tainted the anticipation of Hopper's arrival. Williams notes, "Before [Hopper] arrived, [Robert V.D.] Campbell and [Richard] Bloch had been trying to bribe each other to take the desk next to hers. They had heard that a gray-haired old schoolteacher was coming and neither of them wanted to sit near her." But it didn't take Hopper long to fit in. Her apparel, language, sense of humor, and sarcasm helped the others feel at ease. Williams goes on to write that Campbell and Bloch soon realized their mistake. Hopper was far from the schoolmarm they had imagined. Both men respected Hopper and jumped in to help her gain the necessary programming skills.

Hopper took her assignment to heart. She spent nights examining the blueprints. In his book, *The Innovators: How a Group of Hackers, Geniuses, and Geeks Created the Digital Revolution*, Walter Isaacson quotes Hopper explaining:

> I learned languages of oceanography, of this whole business of minesweeping, of detonators, of proximity fuses, of biomedical stuff . . . We had to learn their vocabularies in order to be able to run their problems. I could switch my vocabulary and speak highly technical for the programmers, and then tell the same things to the managers a few hours later but with a totally different vocabulary.

Innovation requires articulation, and Hopper's strength was her ability to explain computing in a language that could be understood by her peers.

Mark I was a triumph. It was the country's first large-scale digital computer, and it furthered mathematical and scientific research. It added and subtracted in three-tenths of a second. It divided in 14.7 seconds and performed trigonometric functions in eighty-eight seconds. With $250,000 in funding from IBM and a team of programmers and engineers, Mark I was completed in February 1944. It was operational until 1959.

Chapter Three

POSTWAR COMPUTING

The most important problem Grace Hopper and her team had to solve came in the fall of 1944. It was brought to them by the well-known mathematician John von Neumann. He worked for the Manhattan Project, an agency that developed atomic bombs during World War II. Von Neumann was in search of a solution for a highly complicated partial differential equation. This is a mathematical equation that shows how a rate of change—also known as a differential—in one variable is related to other variables. Linn Gilbert, author of *Particular Passions: Grace Murray Hopper*, writes that partial differential equations were "a type that had never before been solved numerically. They required Hopper to call upon everything she had learned from her year of study with [Richard]

Courant in order to translate von Neumann's equations into a working computer program."

In short, von Neumann needed to know two things: how to make a ball implode and where to put the force points around the sphere. Hopper and her team worked tirelessly. A solution arrived in three months. Hopper later learned that they had solved the implosion problem for the bomb that secured a victory over Japan and brought World War II to an end.

The Manhattan Project B Reactor was the world's first full-scale reactor. It produced plutonium for the nuclear bomb that was dropped on Nagasaki, Japan.

THE END OF WORLD WAR II

In the summer of 1944, the Allies were strong. They

pushed against Germany from every direction. Germany finally surrendered on May 7, 1945. However, the war was over only in Europe. It was still very much alive in the Pacific region. Japan refused to surrender. In response, the United States dropped two atomic bombs, one each on the cities of Hiroshima and Nagasaki. Japan finally surrendered on August 14, 1945. By the end, over fifty countries had taken part in the bloodiest war in history.

After World War II, Hopper was in search of her next adventure. With the WAVES program coming to an end, remaining a naval officer wasn't an option. She couldn't become a Harvard professor because, at the time, they did not have female professors. Divorced and without children, she decided to join the Navy Reserve. She helped Howard Aiken establish the Harvard Computation Laboratory, and he put her in charge of Mark I. He even came to her desk one day and told her she was going to write a book. Hopper recounted the incident during an appearance on the television show *Late Night with David Letterman* in 1986: "I said, 'I can't write a book.' [Aiken] said, 'You're in the Navy now.' So I wrote a book . . . the entire manual of the computer." Hopper's five-hundred-page book became the world's first computer programming manual. It offered a history of the mammoth machine, as well as programming guidelines.

Computer pioneer Howard Aiken was famously wrong for believing that only six electronic computers were needed to manage the computing demands of the entire country.

On January 1, 1946, Grace Hopper was promoted to lieutenant. Later that year, her efforts earned her the Naval Ordinance Development Award. Hopper went on to program the Mark II and Mark III.

GOING BUGGY

The common term "debugging" often describes the solving of a technological issue. It was used before World War II, but Grace Hopper helped popularize it. The story is told in a letter written by Hopper. It states:

In the summer of 1945 we were building Mark II; we had to build it in an awful rush—it was wartime—out of components we could get our hands on. We were working in a World War I temporary building. It was a hot summer and there was no air-conditioning, so all the windows were open. Mark II stopped, and we were trying to get her going. We finally found the relay that had failed. Inside the relay—and these were large relays—was a moth that had been beaten to death by the relay. We got a pair of tweezers. Very carefully we took the moth out of the relay, put it in the logbook, and put scotch tape over it.

From that point on, Hopper and her team would

say they were "debugging" the computer whenever Commander Aiken would ask for numbers they didn't have. The moth-in-a-logbook still exists. It was originally placed in the Naval Museum at the Naval Surface Weapons Center in Dahlgren, Virginia. It is now on display at the Smithsonian Institution's National Museum of American History in Washington, DC.

The logbook—with the famous computer moth—is on display. Hopper is credited with coining the term "debugging" while working on the Mark II computer at Harvard University.

ENIAC

In 1946, the Army funded a secret project called the Electrical Numerical Integrator And Calculator (ENIAC). It was the first all-electronic, programmable computer. Its mission was to calculate ballistics tables. These were settings used for target accuracy. Key players in the Ballistics Research Laboratory learned about

THE FOUNDER OF COMPUTER SCIENCE

Alan Turing (1912–1954) was a contemporary of Grace Hopper. He was an English mathematician, cryptographer, and scientist who was credited with developing modern computer science. In fact, he is known as the founder of the field. Like Hopper, Turing had demonstrated an interest in mathematics and science as a youth. After attending King's College, Cambridge, he wrote a paper presenting the idea of a universal machine. It would be able to compute anything that was computable. The machine was known as the Universal Turing Machine. It took ten years, but Turing turned his idea into a design for an electronic computer.

After earning his PhD from the Institute for Advanced Study in Princeton, New Jersey, Turing returned to Cambridge. He worked for the Government Code and Cypher School at Bletchley Park. It was a secret government cryptography unit that broke codes. In July 1939, the Polish Cipher Bureau had shared critical information about the German Enigma machine. This machine was used to code German military and naval signals. A few months later, Turing and a team of mathematicians developed a new machine, the Bombe. It could break the Enigma's messages. This proved vital in 1941 when a German submarine's communication system was cracked. This gave the Allies what they needed to claim an eventual victory over Germany in Europe.

Turing later became fascinated by the concept of artificial intelligence. In 1950, he wrote a philosophical paper called "Computing Machinery and Intelligence." In it, Turing proposed what is known as the "Turing Test." It compared human and machine outputs. Turing died just four years later, but his work inspired generations to continue in the field of artificial intelligence. In 1999, Turing was named one of *Time* magazine's "100 Most Important People of the 20th Century." The article notes, "The fact remains that everyone who taps at a keyboard, opening a spreadsheet or a word-processing program, is working on an incarnation of a Turing machine."

Dr. John W. Mauchly. He'd been conducting research at the University of Pennsylvania's Moore School of Electrical Engineering. Mauchly was brought on board and given the title of chief consultant. Joining him as the chief engineer was John Presper Eckert. He had been a graduate student at the Moore School.

The ENIAC project began on May 31, 1943. The design alone took a year to complete. Then it took another year and a half—and $500,000—to build the machine. After its hardware was put into place, six female computers were asked to program it. They included Kathleen McNulty Mauchly Antonelli, Jean Jennings

The ENIAC had forty panels that were arranged in a U-shape along three walls. It was the most powerful calculating device of its time.

Bartik, Frances Snyder Holberton, Marlyn Wescoff Meltzer, Frances Bilas Spence, and Ruth Lichterman Teitelbaum. These computers did not have manuals, tools, or programming languages to program the ENIAC. They simply used their knowledge, their common sense, and trial and error. Their hard work paid off. They had achieved a nearly impossible task. The six computers hand-routed the needed information through the machine using digit trays, dozens of cables, and three thousand switches. The ENIAC was able to run a ballistics trajectory in seconds. It was presented to the public on February 15, 1946.

The ENIAC itself was physically massive. It spanned 1,800 square feet (9.29 square kilometers) and weighed thirty tons. It was so big, people had to work inside of it. In an article titled "The History of the ENIAC Computer," inventors biographer Mary Bellis notes that the ENIAC was made up of "17,468 vacuum tubes, along with 70,000 resistors, 10,000 capacitors, 1,500 relays, 6,000 manual switches and 5 million soldered joints." Plus, it was a whiz at calculations. When the Mark I calculated three additions per second, the ENIAC could do five thousand per second. Bellis goes on to note:

In one second, the ENIAC (one thousand times faster than any other calculating machine to date) could perform 5,000 additions, 357 multiplications or 38 divisions. The use of vacuum tubes instead of switches and relays created the increase in speed, but it was not a quick machine to re-program. Programming changes would take the technicians weeks, and the machine always required long hours of maintenance.

Bellis writes that after the war, the ENIAC "was still put to work by the military doing calculations for the design of a hydrogen bomb, weather prediction, cosmic-ray studies, thermal ignition, random-number studies and wind-tunnel design." The ENIAC was finally retired in 1955.

THE PRICE OF SUCCESS

Even though women were making their marks in the computer programming industry, it remained a very male-dominated business. Women had social and professional challenges to overcome, and sometimes doing so meant paying a very personal price. This was true for Grace Hopper.

In his book, *Grace Hopper and the Invention of the Information Age*, biographer Kurt Beyer explains, "Hopper, like other women during her era, consciously traded marriage and family for a career. Though she filled the emotional gap with colleagues, Hopper's most common method of dealing with personal loneliness was to throw herself into her work." Understandably, there was a fair degree of pressure involved in being a computing pioneer in a field still in its infancy.

By the 1940s, Hopper's depression was deep. According to Beyer, "close friends and family rescued her from alcoholism and dissuaded her from suicide." Hopper's brush with depression and alcoholism serves as a reminder of the burden that many tech pioneers and innovators face. In many ways, Hopper sacrificed a traditional family lifestyle for the sake of her career. However, her ability to overcome that depression and continue her work in programming and computation only serves to heighten her status as a role model in tech.

Chapter Four

COMPUTERS GO COMMERCIAL

echnological advances made during wartime became appealing for businesses. Improvements meant better functionality, easier user experiences, and the opportunity to make money. Grace Hopper understood this. She recognized that computers were not only important for war efforts, but could also be valuable to a wide range of businesses. But first, computers needed to become more programmer and application friendly.

A RISKY BUSINESS

On August 7, 1946, Hopper was released from active duty. After her time in the navy, she learned that John W. Mauchly and John Presper Eckert had launched a new start-up business in 1946. It was called the Eckert-Mauchly Computer Corporation (EMCC). Its mission was to mass-produce computers and sell them to businesses. Hopper took a professional risk and signed on to work with them in 1949. At the time, the EMCC team was working on the construction of a large-scale digital electronic computer called the UNIVersal Automatic Computer (UNIVAC). Eckert and Mauchly had already designed it in 1947, and Hopper, as head of the software division, was assigned to program it. She hired a team of eight: four men and four women. Some of her recruits were old asso-

John Mauchly (1907–1980) and J. Presper Eckert (1919–1995) stand with the ENIAC. They were honored at the Fall Joint Computer Conference in 1966 for their contribution.

ciates from the Harvard Mark I project, and the others were women from the ENIAC project.

At 25 feet tall (7.62 m) and 50 feet long (15.24 m), the UNIVAC was a technical wonder. It had many parts, including 5,600 vacuum tubes—an upgrade from the electro-mechanical relay switches. The UNIVAC also had 18,000 crystal diodes and 300 relays. With an internal memory, it could manage numbers and alphabetic characters equally. The UNIVAC ran one thousand times faster than the Mark I. It could add in .525 milliseconds, multiply in 2.15 milliseconds, and divide in 3.9 milliseconds. (Milliseconds are a hundredth of a second.) The UNIVAC could isolate complexities regarding large amounts of input and output, namely for data processing applications. As the first computer to have digital magnetic tape, it delivered data at a rate of 40,000 binary digits (bits) per second.

The UNIVAC's development proved to be challenging, though. It needed improvements in design and reliability, and there had been security concerns as well as high development costs. Eckert and Mauchly sold their company to Remington Rand in 1950. The UNIVAC—and Hopper—went with it. The company name changed to the Univac Division of Remington Rand.

THE A-0 COMPILER

Unlike modern-day computers, the computers of yesterday were single, one-of-a-kind units. They had been

COMMERCIAL APPEAL

From 1951 to 1958, forty-six UNIVAC units were installed in various locations around the United States. The Census Bureau used the first UNIVAC computer in June 1951. Prudential Insurance Company was the first business to install one. In 1952, the UNIVAC was also used to accurately predict the outcome of the presidential election between Dwight D. Eisenhower and Adlai Stevenson before the voting polls closed. This prediction happened during a televised news broadcast. At first, no one believed it; but later, the UNIVAC was proved to be very accurate. Eisenhower won the presidency.

Other government agencies and businesses used the UNIVAC, too. These included the Army Map Service in Washington, DC, New York University (for the Atomic Energy Commission), and the University of California's Radiation Laboratory. In 1954, General Electric's Appliance Division was the first to create a payroll application for the UNIVAC. Two years later, the UNIVAC at Westinghouse Electric Company calculated payroll, sales records, and sales analysis.

Remington Rand eventually merged with the Sperry Corporation to form Sperry Rand Corporation in 1955. UNIVAC was purchased as part of the merger. By 1958, forty-six UNIVAC computers had been distributed. The UNIVAC II and the UNIVAC III soon followed. Sperry Rand Corporation later merged with Burroughs and, in 1986, became Unisys Corporation. Today it is a global informa-tion technology company. Unisys offers cloud and infra-structure services, application services, business process outsourcing services, and high-end server technology.

built by small start-ups—such as IBM, Sperry, Fortran, and Remington Rand—and ran independently of one another. They were hardware-specific, as there were no set standards for electronic components, systems architecture, or operating systems. In fact, sharing a common programming language was unheard of. But Hopper envisioned a programming language that could run independently of the unit and communicate with other computers.

By 1952, she created the world's first workable compiler. It became known as the A-0 Compiler. It translated symbolic mathematical code into machine language. This made it easier for nonscientists to write computer programs. Hopper and her team later went on to make improvements, creating the A-1 and A-2. The compilers not only reduced programming costs and processing time, but they allowed programmers to create advanced applications much more quickly. Also, in 1952, the navy promoted Hopper. She was given the rank of lieutenant commander.

Here, the UNIVAC is being prepared to predict the winner of a horse race. The groundbreaking computer also predicted the outcome of the 1952 presidential election.

FLOW-MATIC

Grace Hopper's next big project was to create the first English-language data processing compiler. She thought that programming could be simplified even more. Instead of computers only being able to read binary codes—a series of ones and zeros placed in a certain order that the computer understands—she thought they could be written in English words. She knew that people didn't like symbols and that they much preferred letters. Since letters were symbols, it made sense that computers would be able to recognize them, too. As a result, Hopper and her team developed the B-O compiler. It was later called Flow-Matic.

Flow-Matic made it possible for the UNIVAC—and later the UNIVAC II—to understand twenty English instructions. Some of these included add, compare, execute, jump to, ignore, read, stop, and transfer. *Introducing a New Language for Automatic Programming* details seven benefits of Flow-Matic, from an increased program efficiency and accuracy to increasing the user's skill in systems analysis. The introduction explains that the biggest advantage of the Flow-Matic was that English words made computer programming easier for those who were not scientists. The Flow-Matic helped a wide range of businesses complete tasks, such as payroll calculation and automatic billing. It also laid the groundwork for Grace Hopper's next landmark project: COBOL.

During her time at EMCC, Hopper continued in the Navy Reserves. She was made commander on July 1, 1957.

GRANDMOTHER OF COBOL

Hopper's compilers became the foundation for what is known as the Common Business-Oriented Language (COBOL). It was revolutionary in the field as a computer language for data processors. The theory behind it was that instead of symbols, English words could be used to produce the desired outcome. In fact, it became the cross-platform standardized business language for computers.

Hopper played a key role in COBOL's development. She, along with various computer experts, attended a two-day conference in May 1959. Hosted by the Department of Defense, the conference was called the Conference on Data Systems Languages (CODASYL). Its purpose was to develop a standard programming language that could be used on any computer. Forty representatives arrived at the meeting from government agencies, businesses, and computer manufacturers. Hopper herself represented Sperry Rand Corporation and served as the committee's technical lead. She collaborated with others to create the COBOL language. The specifications were introduced in 1959.

Within ten years, COBOL had become the favorite programming language for business. By the year 2000, approximately 80 percent of all active code used around the world was COBOL. In other words, 240 billion of the 300 billion lines of code worldwide were COBOL. Hopper also directed the creation of COBOL manuals and resources. She later worked for the navy to standardize the use of COBOL and to validate COBOL compilers. Thanks to her extensive work on this project, Grace Hopper earned the nickname the "Grandmother of COBOL."

```
WHEN 3   MOVE WIN-DATA (1:5) TO S-ROAD-
         MOVE WIN-DATA (6:)  TO S-ROAD-
         MODIFY EF-ROAD-HIERARCHY TITLE
         MODIFY LB-ROAD-HIERARCHY-SEC
            TITLE S-ROAD-HIERARCHY-SEC
WHEN 4   MOVE WIN-DATA (1:5) TO S-ROAD-
         MOVE WIN-DATA (6:)  TO S-ROAD-
         MODIFY EF-ROAD-TYPE VALUE S-ROAD
```

Computer code is a specific arrangement of symbolic instructions designed to tell a computer what to do. It is the basis for programming.

SUBVERTING EXPECTATIONS

In 1966, Commander Hopper received a letter from the Chief of Naval Personnel. It requested that she put in an application for resignation. She had reached the twenty-year legal limit for service as a reservist. Hopper did as asked, but admitted that her retirement date, December 31, 1966, was one of the saddest she'd experienced. Hopper continued in her position at Sperry

FAST FORWARD TO Y2K

As the world anticipated the new millennium in 2000, government and business organizations were worried. Their computer programs were not equipped to handle the "rollover." Software programs would read the year 2000 as 1900, due to a computer bug called Y2K. It was a numeronym made up of Y for year, 2 for 2000, and K for kilo, meaning 1000. The bug had the potential to shut down anything that contained a computer system, and people around the world prepared for a total collapse of a high-tech society. Y2K was never an issue until the new millennium approached. For years, programmers had used shortcuts with date math to save valuable memory space.

Many systems used six-digit dates, such as 01/01/85, instead of eight-digit dates, such as 01/01/1985. This worked just fine until the turn of the century. At year 2000, the computer would have difficulty deciding whether it was 1985 or 2085. This could really create a problem if accounts were automatically charged a one-hundred-year late fee!

Date validation was also a concern. For instance, if a shopper used a valid credit card to buy a Ferrari in 1999, the computer would read the card's 01/01/00 expiration date as being "younger" than 1999. The purchase would be denied.

COBOL complicated record keeping. Some programs used a two-digit year. This made it easy to complete pre-printed forms with 19__ as the year. For example, if the year was 1992, the program filled in the blank as 1992. The rollover made these forms say 1900 instead of 2000.

Some COBOL programs that used four-digit dates would generate a form date using the equation $1991 - 1900 = 91$. This was a problem if the year 2001 was used. The computer would produce $2001 - 1900 = 101$ instead of 01.

Six-digit dates weren't helpful either, especially when it came to keeping accurate birth and death records. If a COBOL program entered a person's date of birth as 05/15/96, and that person lived for exactly one hundred years (until May 15, 2096), then its output would record the date of death as 05/15/96. It would be exactly the same, and very confusing.

Programmers around the world worked tirelessly to correct Y2K. The International Y2K Cooperation Center (IY2KCC) was formed in 1988 to reduce the impact of any serious problems. Systems were upgraded, and backup plans were made. When the year 2000 finally arrived, any issues were minor. Since then, COBOL has been replaced by more modern technologies. But there are still some large insurance companies and financial institutions that use COBOL. It would be too costly to replace the account-ing and payroll systems in their dated mainframes.

Rand Corporation. Then in 1967, things looked up. Hopper received word that her naval retirement would be cut short. The computer age had been moving at a faster speed than ever, and her expertise was needed. It took a congressional vote, but Hopper came back to temporary active duty on August 1, 1967. She took military leave from Sperry Rand Corporation and tackled her new job. She was assigned to standardize the navy's use of COBOL and validate COBOL compilers. When her six-month commitment was up, Hopper's orders were changed. The navy wanted her for an "indefinite" period of time. Hopper was delighted.

As Hopper served in the navy, she had to persuade others to think outside the box. Many were stuck, convinced that things should be done as they always had been. According to Hopper's biography on Navy.mil, "On a daily basis, [Hopper] heard someone say, 'But that's how we've always done it.' Hopper believed that change was good, and needed." Hopper herself addressed this attitude, stating that, "In the computer industry, with changes coming as fast as they do, you just can't afford to have people saying that." To further her point, Hopper hung a clock on her office wall that ran counterclockwise. Naturally, this confused visitors. They would check and double-check their watches, confused by Hopper's time-telling ways. She would explain that there doesn't have to be only one way of telling time. Hopper also kept a Jolly Roger skull and crossbones flag on her desk. It represented her piratelike approach to getting what she needed at the Pentagon. Hopper was known to go in late at night to retrieve desired information.

"MAN OF THE YEAR" AND WOMEN'S LIBERATION

Like Hopper, the Data Processing Management Association thought a little differently. In 1969, the organization recognized her pioneering contributions to the data processing industry by giving her the first computer science "Man of the Year" Award. Hopper was delighted and paid no attention to the gender distinction. In fact, she had not participated in the women's liberation movement at all.

The women's liberation movement had its roots in the 1950s. This was a time when the civil right movement pushed for equality for certain minority groups, especially African Americans. Women, too, wanted to be viewed as equals and to be taken seriously. They demanded the same educational and professional opportunities. Women wanted equal promotions and equal pay for their efforts. Furthermore, they wanted to be able to surpass women's traditional roles for historically male-dominated positions. This movement, colloquially referred to as "Women's Lib," gained further momentum in the 1960s and 1970s.

Hopper was unique in her belief that women already enjoyed the same opportunities as males. She believed that if women worked hard, seized opportunities, and approached work with a spirit of collaboration, then they would be viewed as equals. Opportunities would come their way. The fact that Hopper's extraordinary intelligence and work ethic had opened more doors for her than for most women undoubtedly influenced her position. Right or wrong, it was a belief that Hopper carried with her all the way up the naval ladder to her ranking as a rear admiral.

Chapter Five

AMAZING GRACE

Grace Hopper spent the next twenty years of her life standardizing and validating software. She advised the navy on its computing operations and was its most fervent recruiter. She encouraged young people to enlist and to learn computer-programming skills. Hopper was a highly sought-after lecturer. She spoke to military, educational, and business organizations, addressing over two hundred audiences.

RETIREMENT REVISITED

In 1971, a sixty-five year old Hopper retired for a second time. Like before, it was short lived. She was asked to reenlist. The navy thought her irreplaceable. Hopper was promoted to captain on August 2, 1973. That year, Grace

Hopper became the first person from the United States—as well as the first woman worldwide—to become a Distinguished Fellow of the British Computer Society.

That same year, the Univac Division of Sperry Rand established the Grace Murray Hopper Award. This award is given annually to an outstanding young computer professional—age thirty-five or younger—who has made a significant major technical or service contribution. The award comes with a cash prize. In 2014, it was given to Sylvia Ratnasamy, an assistant professor in computer science at the University of California, Berkeley. Ratnasamy was recognized for what ACM.org describes as "contributions to the first efficient design for distributed hash tables (DHT), a critical element in large-scale distributed and peer-to-peer computing systems." Ratnasamy also received a cash prize of $35,000, thanks to funding by Microsoft Research.

The awards continued for Hopper in the 1980s. She was honored with the Navy Meritorious Service Medal for her outstanding contributions. Then, in March 1983, Grace Murray Hopper gave an interview on *60 Minutes*, a popular CBS television show. Millions tuned in, including US Representative Philip Crane of Illinois. Hopper and Crane had never met, but Crane believed that Captain Hopper deserved the lofty appointment of commodore. Crane pushed for a bill in 1983 that would make it so. The House of Representatives approved the bill, and on

November 8, 1983, at the age of seventy-six, Hopper was promoted to the rank of commodore by President Ronald Reagan. The title was later renamed to rear admiral, lower half, in 1985. During her 1986 appearance on the *Late Night with David Letterman* television show, Hopper recalled a moment shared with President Reagan:

[I] got up on my toes and said, "Sir, may I tell you something?" And he looked at me funny as all get out as if I was going to threaten something, and I said, "I'm older than you are." He let out a laugh you could've heard all the way across the country.

US Representative Philip Crane (1930–2014) of Illinois is shown here at a press conference in 1985. He drove the campaign to promote Hopper to the rank of commodore.

THE GRACE MURRAY HOPPER
SERVICE CENTER

On September 27, 1985, ground was broken in San Diego, California, for the Navy Regional Data Automation Center (NARDAC), known today as the Naval Computer and Telecommunications Station. It was home to a 135,577-square-foot (12,595-square-meter) data processing facility, The Grace Murray Hopper Service Center. The Naval History and Heritage Command website describes it as follows:

The building contains a data processing center as well as training facilities, teleconferencing capabilities, telecommunications and expanded customer service areas. A small room-sized museum contains numerous artifacts, awards and citations that Hopper received during her lengthy career. The guest visitor's book contains the names of some prominent people paying homage to the computer pioneer.

RETIREMENT: TAKE THREE

On August 14, 1986, Grace Hopper became the oldest commissioned officer on active duty in the navy. She

Grace Hopper's strides in the field of computer science have inspired generations to pursue their passions in this always-evolving technology field.

officially—and involuntarily—retired in September 1986. Hopper had served a forty-three-and-a-half-year-long naval career. At her request, her retirement ceremony took place aboard the USS *Constitution* in Boston Harbor, Massachusetts. It was the navy's oldest commissioned warship. Three hundred friends and colleagues were in attendance, as well as thirty family members. Hopper's speech focused on the future. The Naval History and Heritage Command's website quotes Hopper as having said that day, "Our young people are the future. We must provide for them. We must give them the positive leadership they're looking for."

Navy Secretary John Lehman honors Grace Hopper during her retirement ceremony aboard the USS *Constitution* in Boston, Massachusetts, in 1986.

The USS *Constitution*, launched in 1797, is the world's oldest commissioned, still-afloat warship.

During the ceremony, Hopper was given the Defense Distinguished Service Medal. It is the highest award given by the Department of Defense. The Air Force Personnel Center explains that the medal is "awarded to the most senior officers whose performance of duties over a sustained period of time are exceptional in nature and directly impact national security or defense at the highest levels. It is the highest peacetime Defense award and is only awarded by the Secretary of Defense." This special medal was one of many honors that Hopper received throughout her career.

A CAREER BEYOND RETIREMENT

A quiet retirement wasn't exactly what Grace Hopper had in mind. In less than one month, she signed on with Digital Equipment Corporation (DEC) as a senior consultant. She continued in this role until 1990. Her job was to represent DEC at industry forums and to serve as a corporate liaison.

In 1986, when asked about her postretirement adjustment to civilian life, Hopper told David Letterman, "They should have a course in civilian dressing. Here I've been wearing nice round-toed flat-heeled shoes, and all of a sudden they want to put me on spike heels, and I fall off." Hopper continued, "I tried to get to some pantyhose; and the first pair bagged at the calf; and the second pair cut me in half; and the third pair did both. How do you get a pair of pantyhose that fit?" The audience was charmed. Just as in her earliest days working in the male-dominated budding computer technology industry, Hopper's wit proved to be her greatest weapon in earning the approval of others.

MAKING IT USER-FRIENDLY

After retirement, Grace Hopper continued to travel on lecture tours across the United States. She addressed audiences at colleges and universities, engineering forums, and computer seminars. She was always sure to encourage industry leaders to welcome change and to avoid the "we've always done it that way" approach to technology. Grace became an admired and recognized leader by all. Her leadership helped her to earn another nickname: "Amazing Grace."

Grace Hopper would also speak to audiences about the early days of computing, the evolution of computer science, the endless drive behind the industry, and where it was headed in the future. She explained that everyone wanted better answers faster and that advances in the field were necessary. Hopper helped her audiences understand this concept with props. A favorite was a foot-long piece of copper wire. She used it to explain the nanosecond.

Nanoseconds are the farthest distance electronic information can travel in one-billionth of a second.

Hopper brought her wire prop to the *Late Night with David Letterman* show in 1986. Being a forward thinker, Hopper brought up the latest development of the era: picoseconds. A picosecond is a thousandth of a billionth of a second, also known as a quadrillionth of a second. To better understand this, she advised the viewers to head for a fast food restaurant to pick up a packet of pepper. The pepper bits inside represented the size of picoseconds. Hopper easily won over Letterman and his audience, but that was nothing new. Hopper was always a crowd pleaser, thanks to her skills as an educator as well as her intellect, wit, and ability to break down complicated computer concepts into user-friendly language. It's no wonder she received so many standing ovations during her lifetime as a speaker.

After forty years of making great strides in the field of computer science, Rear Admiral Hopper considered her greatest accomplishment to be the training of those in the next generation. She was the navy's most fervent recruiter, encouraging young people to enlist and learn computer skills. She spoke to all sorts of people, but her favorite group was made up of youth from the ages of seventeen to twenty. She thought they knew more and were willing to question things. In fact, she thought that working with them was the most important—and most

Coaxial cables are used for data communication. A copper wire is inside the cable, surrounded by insulation, copper mesh, and external insulation.

rewarding—task she'd ever accepted. *In Signals: The Queen of Code*, Hopper says, "We talk about our natural resources. We talk about oil, and coal, and timber. I think we all too often forget that the greatest natural resource we have is our young people. They are our future." Hopper trained and inspired a great number of young men and women who later forged their own way in the field of computer science.

Chapter Six

Grace Hopper: Honored and Remembered

Throughout her life, Grace Hopper was honored with numerous awards, medals, and commendations. For exceptional merit in computer science, she received forty honorary degrees from such prestigious universities as Newark College of Engineering, Long Island University, University of Pennsylvania, and Pratt Institute. Hopper was also recognized in 1985 when the Brewster Academy in Wolfeboro, New Hampshire—the place where her family spent summer holidays—named its computer lab after her. It's known as the Grace Murray Hopper Center for Computer Learning.

Microsoft's Hoppers

In 1990, Microsoft's female team members created a women's group called Hoppers. In an April 2001 profile of the group, Ranae Buscher, a correspondent for *WeNews*'s "Women in Science" column, explained how the organization had grown in its first decade "from a small band of techies e-mailing each other in 1990 within the Microsoft Corporation to a full-fledged Diversity Advisory Council within the gigantic software firm."

Today, the Hoppers group continues to play an important role within Microsoft and works to recruit women employees to the company and retain them. Hoppers offers educational resources and consulting services and also hosts high-profile social events.

The annual Grace Hopper Celebration of Women in Computing encourages women programmers to advance their careers and share their experiences.

The article explains that in the 1980s, Microsoft had a male-dominated company culture in which the earliest computer "geeks" prided themselves on a certain "boy's club" mentality on the job. Buscher explains that, "many of these engineers were skeptical, if not downright dismissive, of their female cohorts' abilities." It was difficult for women to find their place at the table in early computer technology culture, and female colleagues often faced greater difficulties proposing their solutions than their male counterparts. Buscher notes that women faced, "blatant disregard for their opinions and their proposed solutions to technical problems [as well as] exposure to situations that could be construed by many as biased, degrading, or inappropriate."

Therese Stowell, a software engineer, initially had the idea of putting together the group. She teamed up with fellow engineer Teri Schiele, and the two invited other female programmers to join. Participants were free to talk about challenges in the workplace. They also received much-needed support and advice. Hoppers was a huge hit. In 1991, Microsoft officially recognized it as a diversity group, calling it a diversity advisory council. It helped its women participants gain an equal standing with their male coworkers.

Hoppers continues to be an important force in the Microsoft company today. It hosts discussion and study groups touching on various technical topics.

Hoppers has thousands of members across the country and internationally. Membership is open to any female employee as well as contractors and vendors. Microsoft supports Hoppers with computer hardware and server space, an annual budget, and money for its scholarship fund. This fund is used to help young women pursue technical degrees.

HIGHEST HONORS

On September 16, 1991, Grace Hopper was presented the National Medal of Technology. This medal, which was presented to Hopper by then president George H. W. Bush, is considered to be the highest honor of its type in the United States. It is given each year to individuals, teams, or companies that have made long-lasting contributions to the United States' "competitiveness, standard of living, and quality of life" with their technological innovation. Hopper was the first woman to receive the medal as an individual. She was chosen because of her computer programming language achievements. In his speech that day, President Bush said that Hopper "put personal computers on the desks of millions of Americans—and dragged even this president into the computer age." Other recipients of the National Medal of Technology—since renamed the National Medal of Technology and Innovation—include Bill Gates, Steve Jobs, and Steve

Recipients of the National Medal of Technology and Innovation are honored for their contributions that "shape cultural revolutions and world economies."

Wozniak, eBay Inc., The DuPont Company, The Procter & Gamble Company, and 3M.

Just a few months after she received such a prestigious honor, Grace Hopper drew her last breath on January 1, 1992, in Arlington, Virginia. She died in her sleep of natural causes. Hopper was buried with full naval honors in Arlington National Cemetery. This is perhaps the most famous cemetery in the United States. The cemetery serves as the final resting site for "more than 400,000 active duty service members, veterans, and their families." There is certainly no other place Hopper would have wished to be buried.

During her eighty-five years, Hopper was admired as much for her enthusiasm for living and learning as she was for her technological know-how.

In the *New York Times*'s obituary published shortly after her passing, Hopper was noted to be "a self-described 'boat rocker.'" The article highlighted Hopper's professed desire to live until the year 2000. She was quoted as having two reasons: "The first is that the party on Dec. 31, 1999, will be a New Year's Eve party to end all New Year's Eve parties. The second is that I want to point back to the early days of computers and say to all the doubters, 'See? We told you the computer could do all that.'" She may not have lived to see the turn of the millennium, but as usual, Hopper's foresight prevailed.

The National Women's Hall of Fame celebrates the achievements of notable women in the United States. Inductees are examples of imagination, innovation, and inspiration.

Hopper played an influential role in the earliest days of computer technology. She was vital to its evolution and embraced the promising future that it held. She cheered on those who followed in her footsteps and inspired those who would take computer science to the next level. In 1994, Grace Hopper was posthumously inducted into the National Women's Hall of Fame. Her achievements will be remembered, and her legacy will continue.

Ships Ahoy

After Grace Hopper's death, it only made sense that the navy would build a ship bearing her name. The USS *Grace Hopper* (DDG-70) was built by Bath Iron Works in Bath, Maine. It had been commissioned in San Francisco, California, on September 6, 1997. The commissioning ceremony was elaborate, with a military band playing, the American flag hoisted up, and former WAVES proudly commemorating Hopper's legacy. Hopper's younger sister, Mary Murray Westcote, was there to sponsor the ship. Several speakers addressed the hundreds in attendance. Senator Barbara Boxer from California shared that the USS *Grace Hopper* was one of the first ships designed to accommodate both a male and a female crew. In fact, of the 303-member crew, forty-four were women and could perform almost every detail on the ship.

The guided-missile destroyer USS *Hopper* (DDG 70) heads out from Joint Base Pearl Harbor–Hickam, Hawaii, in 2011. It was deployed to the US 5th and 7th Fleet regions.

Rear Admiral William G. Sutton was also there to share a few words. He explained that the USS *Grace Hopper* was equipped with a full range of warfare options. As the US Navy's most advanced guided missile destroyer, it could be a strong presence on the land, in the sea, and in the air. Sutton assured the audience that, "if she's forced to fight, she's built to win."

The ship's motto is the Latin phrase, "Aude et effice." Translated, it means, "Dare and do." In Hopper's entry in Susan Ware and Stacy Braukman's *Notable American*

THE GRACE HOPPER CELEBRATION OF WOMEN IN COMPUTING CONFERENCE

Grace Hopper and her legacy have had a huge impact on women and their growing role in technology. One great example of this is the largest technological conference for women worldwide. The Grace Hopper Celebration of Women in Computing Conference is an annual event that celebrates women role models who have made great strides in computer science and engineering. It also encourages women to connect, collaborate, and explore the next big thing in computer technologies. The conference is a highly anticipated annual event that reassures women in technology that they are not "unicorns." They are a force to be reckoned with and, collectively, can make an impact.

The first Grace Hopper Celebration took place in 1994. Five hundred women attended the first conference. By 2014, attendance had shot up to a whopping eight thousand students and representatives from universities, tech companies, and research lab and nonprofit organizations. They were eager to hear leaders in the computing industry speak on such subjects as technological advances, professional development, software engineering, security, and gaming. The conference also highlights inspirational stories of women in tech. Furthermore, the

Sheryl Sandberg, Facebook's chief operating officer, was the keynote speaker at the 2013 Grace Hopper Celebration of Women in Computing conference.

conference features a career fair for undergraduate and graduate students. Everything that the Grace Hopper Celebration does is to encourage the next generation of female tech pioneers to take their place in the world of computing.

Women: *A Biographical Dictionary,* the majestic ship captured "the spirit of [Rear Admiral] Hopper in her quest for pushing the limits of conventional thinking and looking beyond the norm for innovative solutions and approaches to problem solving." Today, the USS *Grace Hopper's* homeport is Pearl Harbor, Hawaii—the very port whose attack opened the doorway for Hopper's participation in the navy. The USS *Grace Hopper* continues to be one of the most technically advanced ships in the world. And like Grace Hopper, it has traveled the world over, inspiring many.

HOPPER GETS A GOOGLE DOODLE

In 2013, on what would've been her 107th birthday, Google honored the memory of Grace Hopper with a Google doodle. These illustrations are what Google calls "fun, surprising, and sometimes spontaneous changes that are made to the famous corporate logo." They are added to the browser's home page to "celebrate holidays, anniversaries, and the lives of famous artists, pioneers, and scientists." Hopper's doodle features a cartoon drawing of Hopper writing a whimsical COBOL program. It says, "SUBTRACT BirthYear FROM CurrentYear Giving Age." The answer from the computer came back as "107."

The concept behind the popular doodles originated in 1998. Google founders Larry Page and Sergey Brin wanted to do something special to signify their attendance at a conference. As a way to say, "We're out of the office," they tucked a stick figure behind the 2nd "o" in their famous corporate logo. It was simple, but catchy. Fans have looked forward to the illustrations created by a team of artists—also known as doodlers—and engineers. Since then, Google doodles have caught on. Over two thousand Google doodles have popped up on global home pages. Fans have enjoyed everything from postage stamp anniversaries to dragon boat festivals and from the Cricket World Cup to the fiftieth anniversary of the Canadian flag's creation.

Today, Google uses a team of "doodlers" and engineers to bring submitted ideas to life. In fact, those ideas often come from users. If they "reflect Google's personality and love for innovation," the ideas are considered, and possibly turned into the doodles we enjoy today. Ideas are welcome via proposals@google.com. The "doodlers" creating these illustrations follow in the footsteps of many of the figures they honor, including Grace Hopper.

THE HOPPER SUPER COMPUTER

Just as the US Navy honored Hopper with a ship named after her, the National Energy Research Scientific Computing Center (NERSC) honored the tech pioneer with the creation of a state-of-the-art supercomputer. It was named the XE6 Hopper. Supercomputers help scientists gather information and perform a great number of calculations in a short amount of time. The XE6 Hopper is a 153,408 processor-core Cray XE6 system. It makes more than one quintillion calculations per second. Linda Vu of the US Department of Energy explains just how

powerful this computer really is. She writes, "if every person alive simultaneously multiplied one pair of numbers, it would take almost 170,000 planet Earths calculating at the same time to match what Hopper could do in one second." Now that's power! The system was installed in September 2010. **The XE6 Hopper is one of the most powerful supercomputers in the world. It works on important issues, such as global climate change, combustion, and clean energy alternatives.**

Today Hopper's life continues to inspire scientists—men and women alike. Her outstanding lifetime achievements have not only benefited the computer science industry, but also the educational and the military industries. Her work—ranging from programming languages to data processing—was creative, practical, and always colored with the intention of sharing computers with the masses.

In 2010—the year of its installation—Hopper was ranked as the second most powerful supercomputer in the United States and the fifth most powerful worldwide.

83

Grace Hopper was a quintessential pioneer in the technology industry. She had an unrelenting vision and a spirited approach to gadgetry. She worked to do it better and faster, and she always championed the evolution of technology. Her biographer Kurt Beyer writes that, "Hopper's programs mirrored what she held dear, which in her case was the overarching need to help others learn to communicate with these wondrous mechanical creations." Now that's true pioneering.

Timeline

December 9, 1906 Grace Brewster Murray was born in New York, New York.

1924 She graduated from Hartridge School in Plainfield, New Jersey. She reapplied for Vassar College in Poughkeepsie, New York.

1928 Murray graduated from Vassar College with Phi Beta Kappa.

1928–1929 She attended Yale with a Vassar College Fellowship.

1929–1930 Murray attended Yale with a Sterling Scholarship.

1930 Grace Murray earned a masters degree from Yale University.

June 15, 1930 She married Vincent Foster Hopper.

1934 Murray earned her doctorate from Yale University.

December 1943 Hopper was sworn into the navy's WAVES.

May–June 1944 Hopper attended the

Midshipman's School at Smith College in Northampton, Massachusetts.

June 27, 1944 She was promoted to lieutenant junior grade.

January 1, 1946 Grace Hopper was promoted to lieutenant.

August 7, 1946 Hopper was released from active duty. She joined the Harvard Computation Laboratory.

1949 Hopper went to work for Eckert-Mauchly Computer Corporation.

April 1, 1952 Hopper was promoted to lieutenant commander.

1952 She worked for the UNIVAC Division of the Sperry Rand Corporation.

July 1, 1957 Hopper was promoted to commander.

1958 She attends the CODASYL conference.

August 1, 1967 Hopper reported for active duty.

1969 Hopper is declared "Man of the Year."

1971 Hopper retired from the navy for a second time.

1972 The navy asked Hopper to come out of retirement.

1973 Hopper became a Distinguished Fellow of the British Computer Society.

August 2, 1973 Hopper was promoted to captain.

November 8, 1983 Hopper was appointed to commodore, later known as rear admiral, lower half.

September 1986 Hopper retired for the second time from the navy.

1986–1990 Hopper worked for Digital Equipment Corporation (DEC) as Senior Consultant.

January 1, 1992 Grace Hopper died in Alexandria, Virginia.

Glossary

algebra A form of mathematics that uses variables (letters and symbols) in equations.

alma mater An educational institution which one has attended or graduated from.

ballistics trajectory The path of bullets or missiles when in motion.

commissioned officer Those military individuals who have a bachelor's degree and are trained for top leadership roles.

cross-stitch A type of needlework that creates X-shaped stitches.

cryptologist One who studies codes, both in writing and solving them.

dictator A single ruler with complete authority and a reputation for brutal behavior.

diplomacy The skill of being able to deal with others and not cause bad feelings.

draftsman A person who draws plans.

embargo An order by a government to limit trade.

enlisted soldier One who ranks below a commissioned officer and handles more technical aspects of service.

fascist One who prefers a dictator-led political system in which business and labor are controlled by government.

free press The sharing of news that is not controlled by censorship.

geometry A form of mathematics that uses points, lines, angles, solids, and surfaces.

inflation An ongoing increase in the cost of services and goods.

instigator One who causes something to happen.

knot A measurement to determine speed at sea; it is equal to one nautical mile per hour.

mainframe A massive computer that completes multiple tasks at the same time.

needlepoint A type of embroidery made up of counted stitches.

output Energy, power, or information produced by a computer or machine.

schoolmarm A person with strict characteristics that are commonly attributed to old-fashioned schoolteachers.

studious An adjective describing one who focuses on his or her studies.

surveying A skill designed to determine the size, shape, and position of a section of land.

totalitarianism A form of government that is controlled by an unopposed political party.

trade union A group of workers dedicated to the protection of rights and promotion of common interests.

trigonometry A type of mathematics that focuses on functions of triangles and trigonometric functions.

yeomen A naval petty officer who is assigned clerical work.

For More Information

Anita Borg Institute
1501 Page Mill Road, #1105
Palo Alto, CA 94304
(212) 897-2157
Website: http://anitaborg.org
The Anita Borg Institute works to highlight the impact
of women on technology. Its tools and programs
facilitate the recruitment and development of
women in leadership roles in technology.

British Computer Society (BCS)—The Chartered
Institute for IT
BCS, 1st Floor
The Davidson Building
5 Southampton Street
London, WC2E 7HA
England
+44–179–341–7417
Website: www.bcs.org
Since 1957, the BCS has promoted the global IT pro-
fession. It offers training, professional development
services, awards, and an academic community
to its membership of over seventy-five thousand
practitioners, businesses, academics, and students.

Canadian Association of Computer Science (CACS)
Department of Computer Science
University of Calgary
2500 University Drive NW
Calgary, AB T2N 1N4
Canada
(403) 220-8497
Website: http://www.cacsaic.ca
The CACS sets standards for
    computer science across Canada. It represents
    Canadian computer scientists internationally
    and provides outreach materials to youth.

Ladies Learning Code
483 Queen Street West, 3rd Floor
Toronto, ON M5V 2A9
Canada
Website: http://ladieslearningcode.com
Ladies Learning Code is a nonprofit organization
    dedicated to inspiring women and youth to
    become passionate builders of technology.
    It offers skills and resources for a hands-on,
    social, and collaborative experience.

Manhattan Project B Reactor Tour at the Hanford Site
2000 Logston Boulevard
Richland, WA 99354
(509) 376-1647
Website: www.hanford.gov
The Hanford Site, home to the Manhattan Project
    B Reactor, was used by the US government for
    plutonium production in 1943. Tours of the his-
    torical reactor are available to the public.

Phi Beta Kappa
1606 New Hampshire Avenue NW
Washington, DC 20009
(202) 265-3808
Website: https://www.pbk.org
Since 1776, The Phi Beta Kappa Society celebrates
    and advocates excellence in the liberal arts and
    sciences. There are 283 collegiate chapters in
    the United States and sixty active alumni associa-
    tions. Membership is by invitation. Today there
    are over half a million members.

US Navy
1000 Navy Pentagon

Washington, DC 20350

(800) 872-6289

Website: http://www.navy.mil/index.asp

The navy is one branch of the United States' military
branches. Its mission is "to maintain, train and
equip combat-ready naval forces capable of win-
ning wars, deterring aggression and maintaining
freedom of the seas." Most navy missions take
place at sea but can also take place on the land
and in the air.

Vassar College

124 Raymond Avenue

Poughkeepsie, NY 12604

(845) 437-7000

Website: http://www.vassar.edu

Vassar College is a private liberal arts college. Founded
in 1861, it was originally a women's college. It
became a coeducational institution in 1969.

Yale University

Office of Undergraduate Admissions

38 Hillhouse Avenue

New Haven, CT 06511

(203) 432-4771
Website: http://www.yale.edu
Yale University, founded in 1701, is a private
   institution. It consists of the college, the
   Graduate School of Arts and Sciences, and
   thirteen professional schools.

WEBSITES

Because of the changing nature of Internet links,
Rosen Publishing has developed an online list of
websites related to the subject of this book. This site
is updated regularly. Please use this link to access
the list:

http://www.rosenlinks.com/TP/Hopper

For Further Reading

Adams, Simon. *World War II*. New York, NY: DK Eyewitness Books, 2014.

Ambrose, Stephen E., and C. L. Sulzberger. *American Heritage History of World War II*. Boston, MA: New Word City, 2014.

Atwood, Kathryn J. *Women Heroes of World War I: 16 Remarkable Resisters, Soldiers, Spies, and Medics*. Chicago, IL: Chicago Review Press, 2014

Barbier, Franck and Jean-Luc Recoussine. *COBOL Software Modernization.* **Hoboken, NJ: John Wiley Sons, Inc., 2015.**

Beyer, Kurt W. *Grace Hopper and the Invention of the Information Age*. Cambridge, MA: Massachusetts Institute of Technology, 2012.

Brookshear, Glenn, and Dennis Brylow. *Computer Science: An Overview* **(12th Edition). London, England: Pearson, 2014.**

Campbell-Kelly, Martin, William Aspray, Nathan Ensmenger, and Jeffrey R. Yost. *Computer: A History of the Information Machine (The Sloan Technology Series)*. Boulder, CO: Westview Press, 2014.

Cohen, I. Bernard. *Howard Aiken: Portrait of a Computer Pioneer*. Cambridge, MA: Massachusetts Institute of Technology Press, 1999.

Cohen, I. Bernard, and William Aspray, eds. *Makin'*
History: Howard Aiken and the Computer. Cam-
bridge, MA: Massachusetts Institute of Technology
Press, 1999.

Dixon, Chenele. *Something Extraordinary: Parental*
Leadership in Home Education. Victoria, BC,
Canada: FriesenPress, 2011.

Goldsmith, Mike and Tom Jackson. *Computer.* New
York, NY: DK Publishing, 2011.

Hancock, Joy Bright. *Lady in the Navy: A Personal*
Reminiscence. Annapolis, MD: Naval Institute
Press, 2014.

Hardnett, Charles R. *Programming Like a Pro for*
Teens. Boston, MA: Course Technology, 2011.

Isaacson, Walter. *The Innovators: How a Group*
of Hackers, Geniuses, and Geeks Created the
Digital Revolution. New York, NY: Simon &
Schuster, 2014.

Lengyel, Eric. *Mathematics for 3D Game Programming*
and Computer Graphics. Third edition. Boston, MA:
Course Technology, 2011.

Llanas, Sheila Griffin. *Women of the U.S. Navy:*
Making Waves. North Mankato, MN: Capstone
Press, 2011.

Marji, Majed. *Learn to Program with Scratch*. San Francisco, CA: No Starch Press, 2014.

Mee, Jr., Charles L. *1919 Versailles: The End of the War to End All Wars*. Boston, MA: New Word City: 2014.

Payne, Bryson. *Teach Your Kids to Code: A Parent-Friendly Guide to Python Programming*. San Francisco, CA: No Starch Press, 2015.

Sande, Warren, and Carter Sande. *Hello World! Computer Programming for Kids and Other Beginners*. Shelter Island, NY: Manning Publications Company, 2013.

Swayze, Alan. *The End of World War I: The Treaty of Versailles and Its Tragic Legacy*. New York, NY: Crabtree Publishing Company, 2014.

White, Ron. *How Computers Work: The Evolution of Technology*, Tenth Edition. Indianapolis, IN: Que Publishing, 2014.

Williams, Kathleen. *Grace Hopper: Admiral of the Cyber Sea*. Annapolis, MD: Naval Institute Press, 2012.

Bibliography

"About Arlington National Cemetery." Arlington National Cemetery. Retrieved June 4, 2015 (http://www.arlingtoncemetery.mil/about).

"Alan Turing Biography: Educator, Mathematician (1912–1954)." Biography.com. Retrieved June 14, 2015 (http://www.biography.com/people /alan-turing-9512017).

Bellis, Mary. "The History of the ENIAC Computer: John Mauchly and John Presper Eckert." Inventors.about.com. Retrieved June 8, 2015 (http:// inventors.about.com/od/estartinventions/a /Eniac.htm).

Bellis, Mary. "Inventors of the Modern Computer: The Harvard MARK I Computer - Howard Aiken and Grace Hopper." Inventors.about.com. Retrieved March 15, 2015 (http://inventors.about .com/library/weekly/aa052198.htm).

Beyer, Kurt W. *Grace Hopper and the Invention of the Information Age.* Cambridge, MA: The MIT Press, 2012.

Buscher, Ranae. "Inside Microsoft, Hoppers Writing New Code." Womenenews.org. Retrieved June 13, 2015 (http://womensenews.org/story/women -in-science/010413/inside-microsoft-hoppers

-writing-new-code).

Collins, Winifred Quick, and Herbert M. Levine. *More Than a Uniform: A Navy Woman in a Navy Man's World*. Denton, TX: University of North Texas Press, 1997.

"Computing History Displays: Fifth Floor - Harvard Mark 1." The University of Auckland. Retrieved May 31, 2015 (https://www.cs.auckland.ac.nz /historydisplays/FifthFloor/LogicAndSwitching /HarvardMark1/HarvardMark1Pictures.php).

Crowe, Stephanie H. "Preparing for an Apocalypse: Y2K." University of Minnesota. Retrieved June 6, 2015 (http://www.cbi.umn.edu/Y2K/index.html).

"Defense Distinguished Service Medal." Air Force Personnel Center. Retrieved June 8, 2015 (http:// www.afpc.af.mil/library/factsheets/factsheet .asp?id=7727).

Dickason, Elizabeth. "Grace Murray Hopper: Looking Back: Grace Murray Hopper's Younger Years." Originally published by Norfolk Naval Center and *Chips* - The Department of the Navy Information Technology Magazine. Retrieved March 15, 2015 (http://inventors.about.com/library/inventors /bl_Grace_Murray_Hopper.htm).

Dickason, Elizabeth. "Grace Murray Hopper: Remembering Grace Murray Hopper - A Legend in Her Own Time." Originally published by Norfolk Naval Center and *Chips - The Department of the Navy Information Technology Magazine.* Retrieved March 15, 2015 (http://inventors.about .com/od/hstartinventors/a/Grace_Hopper_2.htm).

Dixon, Chenele. *Something Extraordinary: Parental Leadership in Home Education.* Victoria, BC, Canada: FriesenPress, 2011.

Engel, KeriLynn. "Admiral 'Amazing Grace' Hopper, pioneering computer programmer." Amazingwomeninhistory.com. Retrieved June 14, 2015 (http://www.amazingwomeninhistory.com /amazing-grace-hopper-computer-programmer/).

Finley, Klint. "Tech Time Warp of the Week: Watch Grace Hopper, the Queen of Software, Crack Jokes with Letterman." Wired.com. Retrieved June 1, 2015 (http://www.wired.com/2014/10 /grace-hopper-letterman/).

"Frequently Asked Questions (FAQ) About the Y2K Problem." Retrieved June 6, 2015 (http://homepages .wmich.edu/~rea/Y2K/FAQ.html).

Gilbert, Linn with Gaylen Moore. *Particular*

Passions: Grace Murray Hopper. Lynn Gilbert
Inc., 1981.

Google.com. Retrieved May 24, 2015 (https://www
.google.com/doodles/about).

"Grace Hopper Biography." Biography.com.
Retrieved March 12, 2015 (http://www.biography
.com/people/grace-hopper-21406809).

"Grace Murray Hopper." Yale.edu. Retrieved June 14,
2015 (http://www.cs.yale.edu/homes/tap/Files
/hopper-story.html).

"Grace Murray Hopper (1906–1992)." Retrieved
March 15, 2015 (http://www.nwhm.org/education
-resources/biography/biographies/grace-murray
-hopper/).

"Grace Murray Hopper: 9 December 1906–1
January 1992." Naval History and Heritage
Command. Retrieved May 9, 2015 (http://www
.history.navy.mil/research/histories/bios/hopper
-grace.html).

"Grace Murray Hopper Award." ACM.org. Retrieved
June 6, 2015 (http://awards.acm.org/hopper/).

Green, Judy, and Jeanne LaDuke. *Pioneering
Women in American Mathematics: The Pre-1940
Ph.D.'s*. Providence, RI: American Mathematical

Society, 2009.

Hodges, Andrew. "Alan Turing: Creator of modern computing." BBC.com. Retrieved June 14, 2015 (http://www.bbc.co.uk/timelines/z8bgr82).

Hodges, Andrew. *Alan Turing: The Enigma: The Book That Inspired the Film "The Imitation Game."* Princeton, New Jersey: Princeton University Press, 1983.

Isaacson, Walter. "Grace Hopper, computing pioneer." *Harvard Gazette.* Retrieved June 13, 2015 (http://news.harvard.edu/gazette/story/2014/12 /grace-hopper-computing-pioneer/).

"It's In The Hopper: 4,000 Scientific Users Now Working With Supercomputer." Energy.gov. Retrieved June 14, 2015 (http://energy.gov/articles /its-hopper-4000-scientific-users-now-working -supercomputer).

Keating, Anne B., and Joseph R. Hargitai. *The Wired Professor: A Guide to Incorporating the World Wide Web in College Instruction.* New York, NY: NYU Press, 1999.

Markoff, John. "Rear Adm. Grace M. Hopper Dies; Innovator in Computers Was 85." NYTimes.com. Retrieved June 2, 2015 (http://www.nytimes

.com/1992/01/03/us/rear-adm-grace-m-hopper
-dies-innovator-in-computers-was-85.html).

Maranzani, Barbara. "5 Facts About Pearl Harbor
and the USS Arizona." History.com. Retrieved
June 13, 2015 (http://www.history.com/news/5
-facts-about-pearl-harbor-and-the-uss-arizona).

Marx, Christy. *Grace Hopper: The First Woman to
Program the First Computer in the United States.*
New York, NY: The Rosen Publishing Group,
Inc., 2004.

McCann, Allison, "ESPN Films' Signals: The Queen
of Code," Fivethirtyeight.com video, 16:31, January 28, 2015 (http://fivethirtyeight.com/features
/the-queen-of-code/).

Mitchell, Carmen L. "The Contributions of Grace
Murray Hopper to Computer Science and Computer Education." UNT Digital Library. Retrieved
May 25, 2015 (http://digital.library.unt.edu
/ark:/67531/metadc278692/m1/26/).

Myers, Jessica. "The Navy's History of Making
WAVES." Navy.mil. Retrieved May 17, 2015
(http://www.navy.mil/submit/display.asp?story
_id=75662).

"National Medal of Technology and Innovation

(NMTI)." Patent and Trademark Office. Retrieved
June 8, 2015 (http://www.uspto.gov/learning
-and-resources/ip-programs-and-awards).

"Navigating the WAVES in World War II." Naval
History Blog. Retrieved May 23, 2015 (http://
www.navalhistory.org/2014/11/06/navigating
-the-waves-in-world-war-ii).

"1930s News, Events, Popular Culture and Prices."
The People History. Retrieved June 10, 2015
(http://www.thepeoplehistory.com/1930s.html).

"People and Discoveries: Grace Murray Hopper
(1906 – 1992)." Pbs.org. Retrieved June 3, 2015
(http://www.pbs.org/wgbh/aso/databank/entries
/btmurr.html).

Remington Rand Univac: Division of Sperry Rand
Corporation. *Introducing a New Language for Auto-
matic Programming.* Archive.computerhistory.org.
Retrieved June 7, 2015 (http://archive
.computerhistory.org/resources/text/Remington
_Rand/Univac.Flowmatic.1957).

"A Science Odyssey People and Discoveries: Grace
Murray Hopper (1906 - 1992)." Retrieved March
14, 2015 (http://www.pbs.org/wgbh/aso/databank
/entries/btmurr.html).

Sparkes, Matthew. "Grace Hopper honoured with Google doodle." *Telegraph*. Retrieved May 24, 2015 (http://www.telegraph.co.uk/technology /google/google-doodle/10505145/).

Townshend, Charles. "The League of Nations and the United Nations." Retrieved May 30, 2015 (http://www.bbc.co.uk/history/worldwars /wwone/league_nations_01.shtml).

"UNIVAC 1 (1951) First Commercially Available Computer." Computermuseum.li. Retrieved May 16, 2015 (http://www.computermuseum.li /Testpage/UNIVAC–1-FullView-A.htm).

Ware, Susan and Stacy Braukman (Eds.). *Notable American Women: A Biographical Dictionary, Volume 5: Completing the Twentieth Century*. Harvard College, 2004. Cambridge, MA: Harvard University Press, 2005.

Williams, Kathleen. *Grace Hopper: Admiral of the Cyber Sea*. Annapolis, MD: Naval Institute Press, 2012.

"USS Hopper Commissioning (1997) - Part 1." YouTube video, 9:25. Posted by "Naval History and Heritage Command," March 5, 2010 (https:// www.youtube.com/watch?v=_qD5HC_PxfM).

"USS Hopper Commissioning (1997) - Part 2." You-
Tube video, 7:09. Posted by "Naval History and
Heritage Command," March 5, 2010 (https://
www.youtube.com/watch?v=Cd5pEZcM4wU).

"USS Hopper (DDG 70): 'Amazing Grace.'" Navy.mil.
Retrieved March 14, 2015 (http://www.public.
navy.mil/surfor/ddg70/Pages/graceHopper.aspx#
.VQTMJ_zF9qW).

Vu, Linda. "It's In The Hopper: 4,000 Scientific Users
Now Working With Supercomputer." Energy.gov.
Retrieved June 13, 2015 (http://energy.gov/articles
/its-hopper-4000-scientific-users-now-working
-supercomputer).

"World War II Rationing on the U.S. Homefront."
Ames Historical Society. Retrieved June 4, 2015
(http://www.ameshistory.org/exhibits/events
/rationing.htm).

Index

ABOUT THE AUTHOR

After running a successful dance program for over a decade, Erin Staley took her stories from the stage to the page as a writer. Forever a student of the human condition, Erin fostered a passion for history, technology, and the enduring spirit of pioneers in their fields of interest. Today, she writes for the University of California, Riverside, as an international recruitment creative copywriter.

PHOTO CREDITS